WHAT A WASTE

Jess French

DK | Penguin Random House

Project Editor Manisha Majithia
Project Art Editor Sadie Thomas
Editor Kathleen Teece
Editorial Satu Fox, Jolyon Goddard
Design Xiao Lin, Rachael Parfitt Hunt,
Bettina Myklebust Stovne
US Senior Editor Shannon Beatty
Producer, Pre-Production Dragana Puvacic
Producer Basia Ossowska
Senior Producer Isabell Schart
Jacket Designer Anna Lubecka
Jacket Coordinator Issy Walsh
Picture Researcher Sakshi Saluja
Managing Editor Laura Gilbert
Managing Art Editor Diane Peyton Jones
Creative Director Helen Senior
Publishing Director Sarah Larter

Consultant Stephen Burnley

First American Edition, 2019
Published in the United States by DK Publishing
1450 Broadway, Suite 801, New York, NY 10018

Text copyright © Jess French 2019
Copyright in the layouts and design of the Work shall be
vested in the Publishers
19 20 21 22 23 10 9 8 7 6 5 4 3
008–313247–April/2019

A catalog record for this book is available from the Library of Congress.
ISBN: 978-1-4654-8141-2

DK books are available at special discounts when purchased
in bulk for sales promotions, premiums, fund-raising, or educational use.
For details, contact: DK Publishing Special Markets, 1450 Broadway,
Suite 801, New York, NY 10018
SpecialSales@dk.com

Printed and bound in China

A WORLD OF IDEAS:
SEE ALL THERE IS TO KNOW

www.dk.com

contents

Our planet is drowning in waste, but if we act now, it's not too late to save it.

Introduction

As a child, one of my favorite things to do was to search the beach for washed-up treasure. I lived by the coast and spent hours looking through the sand for sea creatures and fossils. I found all sorts of amazing things but, unfortunately, I also found lots of trash. From balloons to toilet seats, I was often more likely to find a piece of plastic than a shell. Today, as a vet, I see first-hand the terrible effect that our garbage has on wildlife and pets.

Humans are now producing more waste than ever before and our planet is suffering. I truly believe that if everyone was aware of how bad their trash is for the planet, they would take steps to change it. By spreading the word, I hope we can begin to turn the tide on waste and make our world a nicer, cleaner place for all of us to enjoy. Luckily, there are simple solutions to many of our waste problems, and the power to make a positive change is in our hands.

Jess French

The problem of waste

We dump enough waste every year to fill a line of trucks going around the world **24 times.**

Building new landfill sites destroys animal habitats, while burning trash creates air pollution.

Throwaway culture

Plastic cups, take-out boxes, spoons, and straws—many products are made to be thrown away! But where do these disposable objects go once you have finished with them?

In 30 years, we'll be creating **70%** more waste than we do now, if we don't change our habits.

Waste is all the things we throw away. Everything we do creates some kind of waste. It's part of living our lives. However, it's important to make sure we don't create more waste than we absolutely have to.

Waste is a problem for animals all over the world. Pets and wildlife can become tangled in plastic litter or mistake parts of it for food. Sea creatures are in the most danger.

As well as attracting disease-carrying rats, huge trash sites called landfills produce gases that warm up the Earth and liquids that pollute water.

Plastic is an amazing material. It is tough, waterproof, and lasts a long time. However, these properties make plastic very difficult to get rid of.

Many types of plastic can't be recycled, and those that get thrown in the trash will not fully rot away.

Pollution

Pollution is when something harmful gets into the environment and hurts animals, plants, and people. It can come from surprising places. Some types of pollution, such as oil in the water, are easy to see, while other types are completely invisible.

Chemicals being sprayed on crops

Soil pollution

Lots of farmers use chemicals to help their crops grow and to kill insects. These build up in the soil and make it poisonous. When it rains, the toxic chemicals get washed away from the soil and end up in local rivers, lakes, and seas.

Water pollution

Oil is a major cause of water pollution. It drips from boat engines, or spills when ships or pipes full of oil are damaged. It sticks to the fur and feathers of sea creatures, which then clump together and stop being waterproof. Animals can be poisoned when they try to get the oil off with their tongue or beak.

Air pollution

Cars, factories, farms, and landfills all create toxic gases. These can spread for hundreds of miles through the air we breathe. Air pollutants are bad for our lungs, causing problems such as asthma.

People drive more than

269 million

motor vehicles in the USA.

250,000
birds were killed in an oil spill from the Exxon Valdez oil tanker in 1989.

Noise pollution

Loud noise is stressful enough to make us ill. One in five people in Europe can hear so much nighttime noise that it could damage their health through lack of sleep. The worst noise villains are cars and aircraft.

Light pollution

The night sky above towns and cities often glows with light. This can be deadly to newly hatched turtles. They mistake the lights for the moon's reflection on water and wander inland instead of out to sea.

92% of the world's people are breathing polluted air.

Air pollution

Of all the different types of pollution, air pollution is the most dangerous. Breathing polluted air kills 7 million people in the world every year. Cities around the world are finding new ways to tackle air pollution.

Electric cars

Cars powered by electricity do not produce as many fumes as cars that run on gasoline or diesel fuel. Diesel is particularly bad for people because when it burns it creates gases called nitrogen oxides, which are dangerous to breathe in.

Researchers have found that **air pollution** makes people worse at math tests.

Greener cities

Planting trees in polluted cities helps to clean up the air. Trees can capture tiny particles of pollution on their bark and leaves, and absorb harmful gases.

Smart warnings

The city of Seoul, South Korea, protects its people by sending warnings if the air pollution is high. This helps people who have breathing problems decide to stay inside.

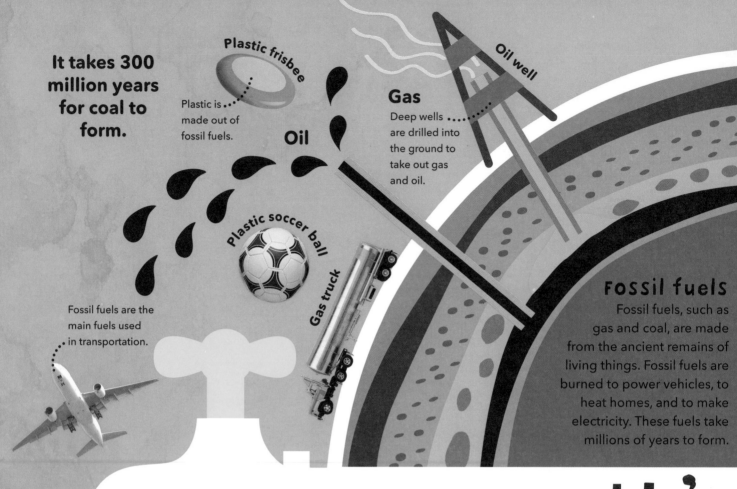

It takes 300 million years for coal to form.

Plastic frisbee

Plastic is made out of fossil fuels.

Oil

Gas

Deep wells are drilled into the ground to take out gas and oil.

Oil well

Plastic soccer ball

Gas truck

Fossil fuels are the main fuels used in transportation.

Fossil fuels

Fossil fuels, such as gas and coal, are made from the ancient remains of living things. Fossil fuels are burned to power vehicles, to heat homes, and to make electricity. These fuels take millions of years to form.

Earth's

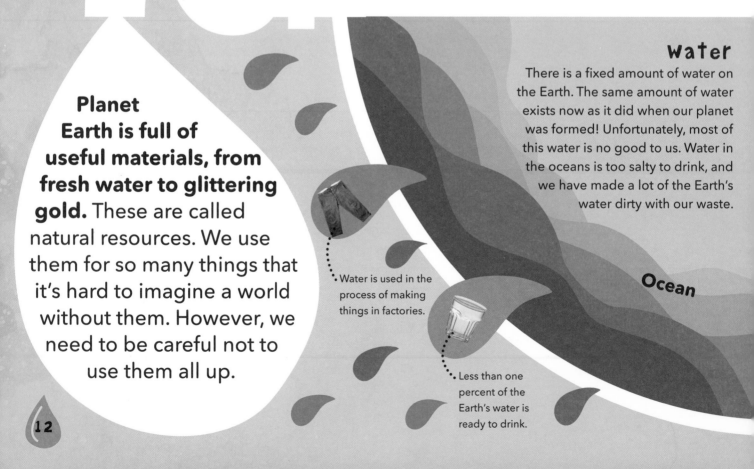

Water

There is a fixed amount of water on the Earth. The same amount of water exists now as it did when our planet was formed! Unfortunately, most of this water is no good to us. Water in the oceans is too salty to drink, and we have made a lot of the Earth's water dirty with our waste.

Planet Earth is full of useful materials, from fresh water to glittering gold. These are called natural resources. We use them for so many things that it's hard to imagine a world without them. However, we need to be careful not to use them all up.

Water is used in the process of making things in factories.

Ocean

Less than one percent of the Earth's water is ready to drink.

Timber forest

Wooden table

More than 60% of the Earth's land was once covered in trees. Now it is less than 30%.

The main reason we chop down trees is for farmland.

Wooden chair

Wood

Wood is an important material. It is used to build houses, make furniture, and as a source of fuel. We also use trees to make books, magazines, and toilet paper.

Wooden spoon

Toilet paper

Book

Forest Stewardship Council (FSC) paper is from forests in which more trees are planted than cut down.

resources

Tin is used to coat other metals to stop them rusting.

Aluminum bike frame

minerals

Minerals are solid materials that form underground over millions of years. There are thousands of different minerals, including silver and gold. Minerals can be valuable, but mining them can greatly damage the environment. We are starting to run out of some rare minerals.

Bauxite is used to make a light, strong metal called aluminum.

Laptop

Tungsten doesn't melt easily and can be found in rockets, laptops, and X-ray machines.

Gold mine

Gold was one of the first minerals to be mined.

Quartz is used in glassmaking.

Glass bottle

An electronic tablet contains around 35 different minerals.

Earth's atmosphere

The ozone layer absorbs up to 98% of the sun's

Greenhouse gases

When energy from the sun hits the Earth's surface, some is absorbed but a lot is reflected back as heat. Greenhouse gases act like a blanket, preventing this reflected heat from leaving the atmosphere. So, if there is an increase in greenhouse gases, the planet becomes warmer. This rise in temperature is called global warming.

Power plant

Power plants generate electricity and many are powered by coal or gas. When these fuels are burned, they release large amounts of carbon dioxide. This is the greenhouse gas most commonly produced by human activities.

Ozone is a form of the gas oxygen. The ozone layer is high up in the atmosphere.

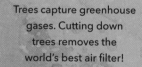

Trees capture greenhouse gases. Cutting down trees removes the world's best air filter!

Transportation

Cars, trucks, buses, trains, and planes give off huge amounts of greenhouse gases. This is because most of these vehicles are currently powered by burning fossil fuels.

A single cow can release up to

265lb

(120kg) of the greenhouse gas methane each year.

The atmosphere is a layer of gases surrounding our planet that protects us from the sun's heat. Gases that keep the Earth warm are called greenhouse gases. Activities such as burning fuel to power vehicles produce more of these. This causes a rise in temperature all over the world.

UV rays, which damage skin.

Extreme weather

Global warming causes extreme weather. In recent years, heatwaves, droughts, wildfires, and rain and snow storms have become much more common.

Melting ice

Rising temperatures across the world are causing large areas of ice, such as mountain glaciers, ice caps, and ice sheets in polar regions, to melt. The resulting meltwater flows into the ocean, raising the sea level.

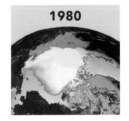
1980

2012

Sea ice covering the Arctic Ocean is shrinking. Look at the amount of ice in the summer of 1980 (left) compared with the amount in the summer of 2012 (right).

Smog

Smog is a thick fog of toxic gases and particles, usually found over cities. It is worst on hot days when there is no wind to carry it away.

Coastal areas are most at risk from rising sea levels due to melting ice.

Extreme weather can cause problems such as flooding.

Hot weather and low rainfall increase the risk of dangerous wildfires.

Deforestation

Humans have been cutting down trees for thousands of years to build homes and make fires. We are now cutting down forests faster than ever before, not only for timber and fuel but also to clear large areas for farming. Trees are also cut down to make paper—we use 985,000 tons (1 million metric tons) of paper every day!

Orangutans have lost more than 80 percent of their forest habitat in the last 20 years. They are now at high risk of extinction in the wild.

Palm oil

Palm oil is a smooth, creamy oil made from the fruit of the African oil palm tree. It is used in a huge number of products, from cooking oil and chocolate to cleaning products and lipstick. The oil palm tree is native to Africa, but it's now grown in other parts of the world on huge farms called palm oil plantations. Forests are cut down and replaced with palm oil trees, and that means animals lose their homes.

Palm oil fruit

There are 3 trillion trees in the world, but **15 billion** are cut down every year.

WHAT CAN YOU DO?
Ask your parents or caregivers to choose products that use sustainable palm oil. This means the oil palm trees have been grown in a way that is kind to people, animals, and their environment.

Palm oil is used in more than half of all packaged supermarket products.

Palm oil is a preservative, which means it stops things from spoiling. It has many other names—at least 200! They include palm kernel, palmate, glyceryl, stearic acid, sodium kernelate, and often it is just referred to as vegetable oil. So, it can be very difficult to know if your favorite products contain the oil. However, if you really want to avoid it, you can do some research on the internet to find brands that make a point of not using it.

Why do we need forests?

Forests are not just a collection of trees—they are a vital part of a healthy planet.

Carbon dioxide As trees grow, they use up carbon dioxide, a gas in the air that causes climate change. They soak up other harmful gases from the air, too.

Oxygen Forests are the "lungs" of the Earth, pumping out the oxygen that we breathe.

Water supply Trees transport water from the soil back into the air, where it can form rain clouds that prevent droughts.

Soil protection Tree roots keep the soil in place, preventing it from being carried away by water or the wind.

Flood protection During heavy rainfall, trees slow the flow of water into rivers and streams, helping to prevent floods.

Medicines Lots of medicines are extracted from rain forest plants or based on substances found in them.

Biodiversity About 80 percent of all living things found on land live in forests. This variety of life is called biodiversity.

People About 300 million people worldwide live in forests, and even more depend on them for their work and food.

17

Conservation

Many types of animal and plant are threatened by human actions, such as deforestation, hunting, pollution, climate change, and disease. We have to act now to protect them and make sure they do not disappear forever. There are many ways we can help threatened species.

Reintroductions

We can help animals that find it hard to survive in the wild by breeding them in captivity. In eastern Asia, Amur leopards struggle in the wild. However, we are now breeding them in zoos in the hope they can one day go back to their natural home.

Amur leopard cub

Protecting our oceans

If we make overfished parts of the oceans into protected areas, the numbers of fish there will get a chance to recover. The Rapa Nui Rahui Marine Protected Area, off the coast of Chile, protects more than 140 marine species found nowhere else on the Earth.

Extinction

Many animals have smaller and smaller spaces to live in due to deforestation, destruction of their habitats, and hunting. If we don't protect them and their natural homes, they will soon die out, just like the dodo.

Dodo

Ecotourism

Trips to areas where there are endangered animals and habitats is called ecotourism. It brings in money to local communities and helps protect wildlife. Tourists have to be careful not to cause any harm. They must keep to footpaths and not get too close to the wild animals.

Protecting our forests

The best way to protect forests is to turn them into conservation areas. In 2017, Papua New Guinea created the Managalas Conservation Area, protecting 1,400 sq miles (3,600 sq km) of ancient forest.

Reintroducing animals to their habitat once they have been wiped out can be very difficult. However, in 2009, beavers were reintroduced to Scotland, UK, and they are doing well!

Rhino horn

All over the world, animals are killed for their body parts. Rhinos are killed for their horns, which are used in traditional medicine. In some places, vets remove rhinos' horns, so that poachers have no reason to kill them.

Black rhino

A rhino in South Africa has its horns sawn off to make it "valueless" to poachers.

Amazing sea creatures, such as porpoises and dolphins, can be injured or killed by fishing nets. In 2017, Mexico banned the gillnet. This kind of net was threatening to wipe out a type of porpoise called the vaquita.

Vaquita

Hunting bans

In some areas, animals are still hunted and killed for sport. Grizzly bears are one of the animals targeted in this way. In 2017, British Columbia, Canada, banned the killing of grizzly bears for either meat or sport.

Grizzly bears are a "keystone species"—meaning they are crucial to the well-being of their ecosystem.

Renewable energy

Life would be very different without heating and electricity.
We are using up fossil fuels to create these types of energy, and we can't make more of them. Energy from sources that will never run out is called renewable energy!

Greenhouse gases surround the Earth, making it warmer. These gases are produced when fossil fuels are burned to make energy.

Biomass

Plants can be used as fuel. Crops, leftover food, wood, and waste can be burned to make energy.

Solar

Light energy from the sun can be used to heat water and to make electricity. It is collected by solar panels.

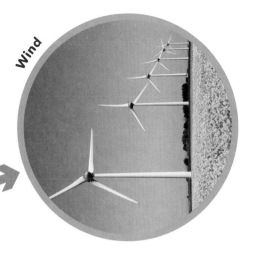

Wind

Wind power is collected using wind turbines. The wind turns their blades, setting off machinery that changes the energy into electricity.

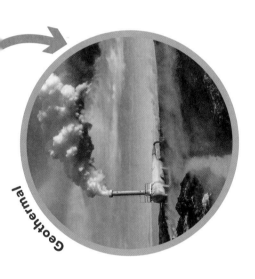

Geothermal

Rocks and water deep underground are hot, or geothermal. This heat can be used to create electricity.

Hydroelectric

Hydroelectric energy uses the power of moving water. Dams are built to direct river water so that it drives electricity-making machinery.

New technology

Scientists are working to develop new and exciting ways of producing energy that will not harm the planet.

Human-heated buildings

Using renewable energy means better air and healthier lungs.

Human warmth can be used to heat buildings! Body heat in busy buildings can be collected in air vents. It warms up water to be pumped through pipes.

Electric cars

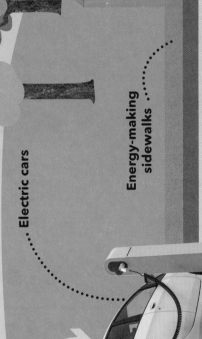

Cars can run on electricity instead of gas or diesel, which are fossil fuels.

Energy-making sidewalks

Special sidewalks can create power! Footsteps press down on machinery beneath the sidewalk, which produces energy for things such as lighting.

Efficient home

Many homes lose heat, waste water, or use too much electricity. Efficient homes waste very little or nothing! Their electricity and heat is often made without using fossil fuels. In homes that aren't specially built to be efficient, there's lots that can be done to waste less.

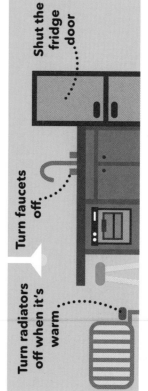

Solar panels Solar panels change sunlight into electricity.

Solar phone charger Electrical items can be powered by the sun.

Take shorter showers

Close windows Homes lose lots of heat through their windows.

Turn radiators off when it's warm

Turn faucets off

Shut the fridge door

Turn off the TV Turn this off after use, or read a book instead!

Turn lights off in empty rooms

Earthships

These homes provide their own energy and collect water from rain.

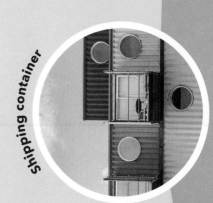

shipping container

Containers used for shipping cargo can be made into homes.

Double glazing
Less heat transfers to the outside with these windows.

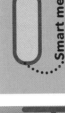

Energy-efficient light bulbs
These are cheaper to run than normal bulbs.

Insulation in walls
Heat is lost through walls. Special padding called insulation can be used to keep it in.

Smart meter
This allows you to keep track of the energy you use.

Washing machine
These can wash clothes using hot or cold water. The cold setting saves energy.

Renewable energy makes up around 18% of the world's energy!

zero carbon

A system that does not produce carbon dioxide is called "zero carbon."

Dirt is used to build some eco-houses!

straw-bale house

Bales of straw are good insulators and can be used to build houses cheaply.

Eco-houses

An eco-house is built to have a small effect on the environment, and is often made out of reused or natural materials. It is very well insulated and airtight to keep heat in. The electricity comes from renewable sources, such as sunlight.

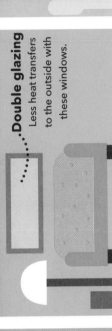

Household waste

Almost everything we do creates waste. From leftover food and broken belongings to packaging and old clothes, we often throw away things that could be mended or reused. If we recycle trash instead, it will be made into something new. However, many things can't be recycled.

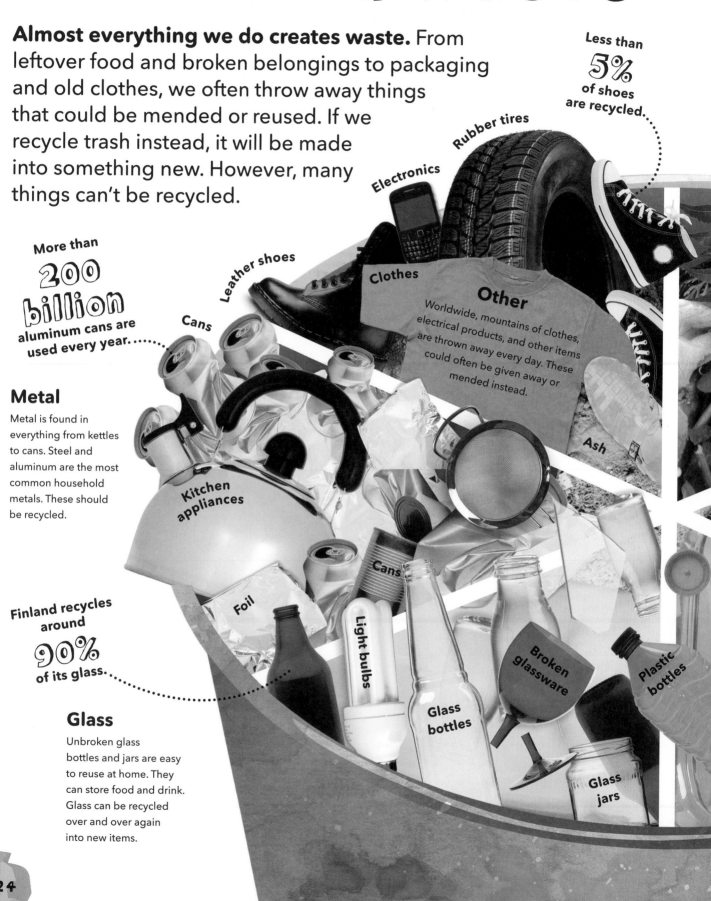

Less than **5%** of shoes are recycled.

Electronics

Rubber tires

Leather shoes

Cans

Clothes

Other
Worldwide, mountains of clothes, electrical products, and other items are thrown away every day. These could often be given away or mended instead.

Ash

More than **200 billion** aluminum cans are used every year.

Metal
Metal is found in everything from kettles to cans. Steel and aluminum are the most common household metals. These should be recycled.

Kitchen appliances

Cans

Foil

Light bulbs

Broken glassware

Plastic bottles

Finland recycles around **90%** of its glass.

Glass
Unbroken glass bottles and jars are easy to reuse at home. They can store food and drink. Glass can be recycled over and over again into new items.

Glass bottles

Glass jars

Some places around the world are trying to create zero, or no, waste. Keep reading this book to see how you can create less waste!

Around **24 million** slices of bread are thrown away from UK households every day!

Garden waste

Food scraps

Food and garden

Huge amounts of food are wasted worldwide. Garden waste, such as plant cuttings, also gets thrown away.

Wrapping paper

Cardboard

Each year, most US households throw away **13,000** pieces of paper.

Newspaper

Paper

We have been recycling paper for thousands of years. Sadly, lots of paper is put in trash cans and doesn't get recycled.

Packaging

91% of all plastic ever created has not been recycled.

Containers

Plastic

Billions of plastic items are thrown away every day. Some types can be recycled. However, the process is difficult, and plastic can only be recycled a few times.

Did we always throw away this much?

In the past, people created much less waste. It was only in the 20th century that we first began to throw away so much. So what changed?

Furniture

Rags

Bones

1900

Things were often expensive or homemade. Old items were reused or fixed. Only things that were beyond repair were thrown away.

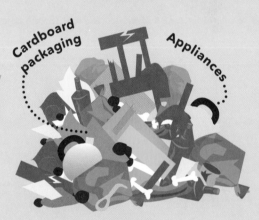

Cardboard packaging

Appliances

1950

Plastic packaging had not yet been invented so cardboard was used instead. Most electrical items were expensive and rarely thrown away.

Plastic

Clothes

Present day

Many things are wrapped in plastic packaging. It is cheap to make clothing and electronics, so we buy more than ever and throw lots away.

where does it go?

When you throw something away, it might end up on the other side of the world! All waste goes on a journey after it's put in the trash. Whether by foot to a recycling bank or by truck to a landfill, waste is taken away to make new things, to help plants grow, or to be burned or safely disposed of.

General waste

This type of waste cannot be recycled or composted. General waste is taken by garbage trucks to different sites.

The truck crushes the trash so that it takes up less space.

Recycling waste often gets transported by truck too.

Recycling containers

What can go in recycling containers depends on where you live. Some places have receptacles for each material. Other places have mixed containers.

Organic waste

Garden waste and some food waste break down into a brown mixture, called compost. This waste can also be broken down into a gas by microbes and used to make electricity.

Incineration plant

The waste is usually taken to one of two destinations.

Here, trash is burned. The burning trash heats water into steam that powers machinery to make electricity.

Landfill

Landfill sites are also known as dumps. They are holes in the ground where waste is buried. They can cover huge areas.

Oil in food can stain packaging to make it unrecyclable.

Recycling plant

Recycling is sorted into different types of material and made into new items. Unrecyclable items are sent to be incinerated or to landfill.

Sent abroad

From 2014 to 2016, the UK sent 881,849 tons (800,000 metric tons) of plastic waste a year to be recycled or disposed of in other countries.

Growing plants

Compost can be spread over fields and gardens to help plants grow. Some cities collect compostable waste to make compost.

Hazardous

Items such as batteries contain hazardous, or harmful, materials. These go into special cans to be disposed of safely.

Landfill

As waste decomposes, or breaks down, harmful gases such as methane and carbon dioxide are produced.

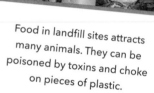

Food in landfill sites attracts many animals. They can be poisoned by toxins and choke on pieces of plastic.

Water trickling through landfill (leachate) collects toxic particles and can poison nearby groundwater (water under the ground).

As human populations grow, people are living closer to landfill sites. This can be a serious health risk.

  Bantar Gebang landfill site in Jakarta, Indonesia, is one of the 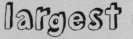 **in**

Massive trash piles are known as landfill sites. Many years ago, people just threw any waste out into the streets. Eventually, we realized that living next to trash was bad for our health. It caused illnesses, so we began to move our waste out of cities and towns to landfill sites.

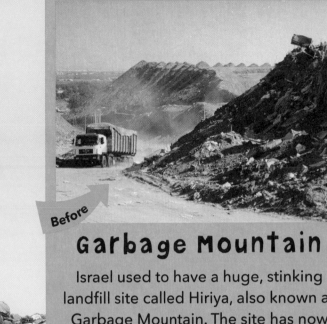

Before

Garbage Mountain

Israel used to have a huge, stinking landfill site called Hiriya, also known as Garbage Mountain. The site has now been transformed into Ariel Sharon Park. The mountain of trash was sealed with a layer of plastic. On top of this, gravel and soil were added so that plants could grow. Other countries are now doing the same with their old landfill sites.

After

Dangerous gases can be produced in landfill sites if chemicals such as ammonia and bleach mix together.

Visitors to the park can go on walking and cycling trails, visit its small zoo, and enjoy outdoor concerts.

the world and the same size as **160 soccer** fields.

Plastic forever

Once a plastic object such as a toy or water bottle is made, it sticks around for a very long time. Plastic does not rot away, it just breaks down into smaller and smaller pieces. We have to find somewhere to put all the plastic objects we throw away.

where does it go?

9% of plastic is recycled.

12% of plastic is burned.

79% of plastic is buried in landfill or dumped on land or at sea.

Since plastic was invented, around 9.1 billion tons (8.3 billion metric tons) have been made. A lot of this plastic goes into trash dumps called landfill sites. Only a small amount has been recycled so far.

Types of plastic

There are many types of plastic, each with different properties—from strong and hard to soft and flexible. We need to make sure we dispose of them correctly. Some plastics cannot be recycled, while others can only be recycled in centers that have the correct technology available.

Polyethylene Terephthalate (PET)

This is one of the most common types of plastic used to make things. It is found in most water bottles and drink bottles. Plastic containing PET can be widely recycled but should not be reused because bacteria can start to grow on it over time. Also, chemicals from within the plastic could start to leak into the contents.

Plastic bottle

Polystyrene (PS)

This is a lightweight and easily made plastic, generally used to make disposable drinking cups, egg cartons, and foam packaging. It breaks up easily and is often blown into oceans, where it can harm marine life. Polystyrene cannot usually be recycled and we should reduce our use of it wherever possible.

Polystyrene cup

Polypropylene (PP)

This plastic is tough, light, and heat-resistant. It is used to make plastic liners found in cereal boxes, disposable diapers, yogurt containers, and chip bags. PP can sometimes be recycled but isn't accepted everywhere. To recycle items made from PP, always check if your local recycling center will accept it.

Disposable diaper

How can I help?

- Drink from a reusable water bottle instead of disposable plastic bottles.
- Use paper straws and cups, and wooden cutlery, rather than plastic.
- Take your own bag to the supermarket rather than using a new plastic one.

Around 20,000 plastic bottles are bought per second. Less than half of these are collected for recycling.

Single-use plastic

Plastic milk jugs

Plastic drink bottles

Plastic cups

Throwaway items

Not including incinerated waste, almost every single piece of plastic ever created still exists! Plastic never breaks down entirely, just into smaller and smaller bits. About 40 percent of plastic is unneeded packaging.

Soap bottle

Plastic toothbrushes

Disposable diapers

Balloons

When balloons fall back down to the Earth, they are often eaten by wildlife. This can make animals ill.

Sea turtles often eat plastic bags, confusing them with jellyfish. The turtles' digestive systems can become blocked with plastic.

Plastic straws

Plastic cutlery

Plastic wrap

Enough plastic is thrown away each year to wrap around the Earth **four** times.

Plastic bags are used for an average of **12** minutes.

Plastic packaging

We live in a disposable world. Half of all plastic items are used just once before being thrown away. Put together, this would create a pile of waste weighing about the same as three Empire State Buildings.

Milk to refill a reusable milk bottle

Reusable cups

60 million disposable water bottles are thrown away every day.

Reusable bottles

Eco-friendly swaps

You can swap environmentally friendly or reusable materials for every single type of disposable plastic. Natural materials that break down without causing pollution, such as mushrooms, make great packaging. Some people try not to create any trash at all!

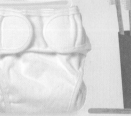
Reusable diapers   **Wooden toothbrushes**

Bars of soap

Plastic wrap is made of plastic, but beeswax wraps are a reusable alternative.

Fresh, loose fruit and vegetables

Metal cutlery

Paper straws

Plastic straws take up to **200** years to break down into tiny pieces.

Beeswax wrapping

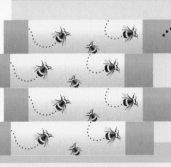

Mushroom Packaging   **Pasta to refill your reusable containers**   **Tote bag**

Save our seas!

Imagine an island of trash in the middle of the ocean. When plastic items get washed into the sea, they clump together and form floating trash dumps. Plastic breaks down so slowly in water that it may never entirely disappear.

Hard hats have been found in the oceans dating back as far as

1989.

Asia

Pacific Ocean

island of trash

Garbage in the oceans is carried by moving water until it forms gigantic floating trash patches. The biggest of these patches is the Great Pacific Garbage Patch (GPGP), which is in the north Pacific Ocean. It is about three times the size of France and contains around 1.8 trillion pieces of trash.

Sea turtles caught in the Great Pacific Garbage Patch can end up with

74%

of their diets made up of ocean plastic.

Australia

The plastic in the GPGP weighs around the same as 500 jumbo jets!

North America

Ocean gyres

Ocean water moves in patterns called currents. Gyres are currents that move around in a circle. They collect pieces of trash into huge swirling patches of waste. There are five main garbage patches in our oceans.

Microplastics have been found dating from the **1950s**.

Almost half of the trash in the Great Pacific Garbage Patch comes from discarded fishing nets.

Microplastics

Plastic in the sea never fully disappears but only breaks down into smaller pieces. Pieces of plastic less than 0.2in (5mm) are called microplastics. Fish and birds mistake these pieces for food and eat them.

Many organizations are helping to clean up ocean garbage, such as the ones below. Ask an adult before becoming a litter-picking hero too!

cleaning up our oceans

From straws to deflated footballs, around a third of the plastic made each year ends up in oceans and on beaches. So what can we do to help? Scientists, governments, and ordinary people are trying to tackle this problem.

Take 3 For The Sea

Become part of this project by taking just three pieces of trash away whenever you leave a beach or waterway. Make sure recyclable materials are recycled!

Coastal Cleanup Day

Join volunteers across more than 100 countries for a beach cleanup on International Coastal Cleanup Day. This is in mid-September every year.

The world's largest cleanup

The largest beach cleanup in history took place on Versova beach, Mumbai, India. Over a three-year period, a team of volunteers managed to remove nearly 22 million lb (10 million kg) of trash from the beach.

Before

After

The ocean-cleaning machine

The Ocean Cleanup organization's plastic-gathering machine is the first of its kind. It has been designed to remove 50 percent of the waste in the Great Pacific Garbage Patch within five years. It will gather the plastic waste together, so that it can be removed by nets and brought back to land to be recycled.

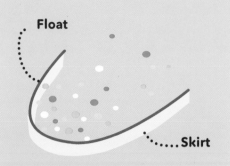

Float

Skirt

A U-shaped float sits on the ocean's surface. A large "skirt" is attached to the float, beneath the surface of the water. The plastic-gathering machine slowly moves forward to gather plastic.

#2minutebeachclean

The next time you're on a beach, become part of this project by taking two minutes to collect as much trash as you can.

Organize your own!

Cleanups show just how much waste we are making. Get your friends and family together for your very own project and help spread the word about waste!

Help stop ocean garbage

Around 80 percent of ocean plastic is from land. There are things you can do to help stop litter getting into oceans.

Litter can be blown into a river that then carries it to an ocean. We can help stop this by securing trash in garbage bags and not littering.

Wet wipes that are flushed down the toilet can end up in the ocean. Wipes that break down in nature can be used instead.

Waste in landfills can blow into rivers. It's helpful to use less plastic and recycle what you can!

Around 75 million tons (68 million metric tons) of waste are thrown away daily.

Save the world with the 3 Rs.

1 Reduce

The best way to stop creating so much waste is to buy fewer things. Take a tote bag to the store instead of using plastic bags and buy loose fruit and vegetables to avoid too much plastic packaging.

2 Reuse

The next best thing you can do is reuse things instead of only using them once. Try a craft project to find new uses for old things. Cans and jars make great storage containers, while colorful paper can be used to wrap presents.

3 Recycle

For everything else, recycle as much as you can. Plastic is particularly difficult to recycle, so make eco-friendly swaps like using a paper bag that can be recycled in place of a plastic one that can't.

Many people are trying to live Zero Waste lives. Some of them can fit their trash from a whole year inside a single jar jar!

Environmental experts say waste that cannot be reused at home should be recycled. This means the materials are made into new items, saving the use of new materials. However, not all waste is recyclable.

24 trees go into 1.1 tons (1 metric ton) of newspaper.

Poop gets given new life!

Recycled trash can turn up in the most unlikely of items. From bike tires to notebooks, your belongings could be made of old spoons or even poo!

Plastic bottle

Glass jar

Metal spoon

Chewing gum

Cardboard

Elephant poo

Tire

Notebook

Fleece jackets

Toilet paper

Bike frame

Astro turf

Japan was the first country on record to recycle paper. In as long ago as **1031 BCE,** all paper was

Germany tops the recycling tables

The top five recyclers in the world manage to recycle over half of their waste.

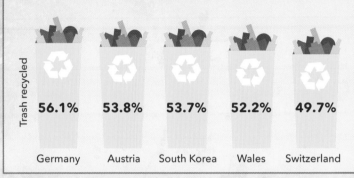

Trash recycled				
56.1%	53.8%	53.7%	52.2%	49.7%
Germany	Austria	South Korea	Wales	Switzerland

Germany made history

In 1991, Germany became the first EU country to make people producing goods responsible for recycling their own waste packaging.

Ban on bags

California banned the giving away of plastic bags in stores in 2015. It was the first US state to do so.

Bacteria eats plastic

Plastic can only be recycled a few times because it loses quality with each round. However, scientists may have found a way to get rid of leftover plastic. A bacterium that eats the type of plastic often used to make disposable bottles was discovered in 2016. The bacterium, called *Ideonella sakaiensis*, breaks the plastic down and uses it to help itself grow.

Recycling offenders

Many everyday materials cannot be recycled. These include chip bags, tissue paper, and certain types of plastic. Food-stained items are also non-recyclable.

recycled and re-pulped into new paper.

Recycling paper

Millions of trees grown on plantations and from forests are cut down every year to make paper for books, newspapers, magazines, and for drawing or printing on. Recycling paper saves these trees.

1 The paper is mixed with water to produce a slurry, or sludge. This is the first stage of de-inking, during which any ink is removed.

2 The slurry is moved through cleaning screens to remove stains, such as ink.

3 Air is pumped in. Ink attaches to the bubbles and floats to the top, where it is removed.

4 The slurry is filtered through screens again. This removes things such as glue and staples.

5 The pulp is bleached white and then pressed into sheets and cut to size.

Use less, waste less

Although it's good to recycle, the process still uses energy to turn waste into something new. It's much better—and more fun—to reuse your old things and turn them into something new and exciting. This is called upcycling, and its possibilities are endless!

Before you throw it away, think creatively and reuse!

Old plastic bottles can be turned into loads of useful objects, such as bird feeders, plant pots, and funnels.

In medieval times, armor was reused for centuries!

A great way to reuse is to buy second-hand items. Something you need might be in your local charity shop.

You could run a swap shop and trade clothes with your friends. How's that for a free makeover!

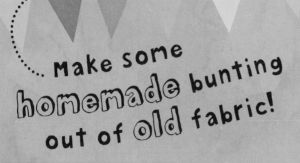

Make some homemade bunting out of old fabric!

Give a glass jar a new life

Jam jars and other glass jars make great containers for pens and other items of stationery. You can also use them as drinking glasses or paint them with glass paints to make colorful candle holders.

Printed wrapping paper

Leftover paper or cut-up old clothes can be made into wrapping paper. Use stamps to print on the paper or cloth—you can even make your own stamps out of old sponges or potatoes.

Designing your own wrapping paper adds a special touch to a gift.

Parcel

Instead of buying new...

Need a tote bag? Don't throw out your old T-shirts! Instead, follow these easy-peasy steps to make an eye-catching accessory.

You will need: scissors and an old T-shirt

Be careful with scissors. Ask an adult to do the cutting for you.

1
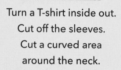
Turn a T-shirt inside out. Cut off the sleeves. Cut a curved area around the neck.

2
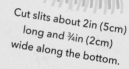
Cut slits about 2in (5cm) long and ¾in (2cm) wide along the bottom.

3

Double-knot front and back strands.

4

Decorate your bag with a patch.

Turn right side out.

Sewing skills

In the past, people were taught to make the most of what they had. More people had sewing skills, so they could fix any holes or loose seams in their clothes.

From trash...

Once you have finished using something, it doesn't stop being useful. Many people have found creative new ways to reuse their trash. The Cateura community in Paraguay live near the largest landfill site in the country. They have formed an orchestra that plays instruments made from garbage found in the landfill site.

How can you help? Get creative! **Why not turn your own trash into treasure?**

to treasure

Recycled Orchestra

The Orchestra of Recycled Instruments of Cateura was founded in 2006 by Fávio Chavez. It is formed of 30 children, whose instruments are made from items of trash that have been reshaped and put together. The instruments include violins, saxophones, and drums. The group have inspired similar programs in Brazil, Ecuador, Panama, and Burundi.

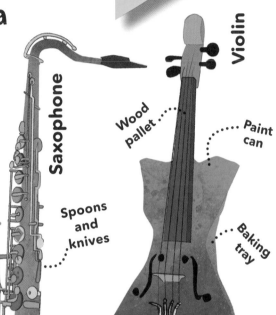

Saxophone

Water pipe

Spoons and knives

Buttons

Bottle tops

Violin

Wood pallet

Paint can

Baking tray

Fork

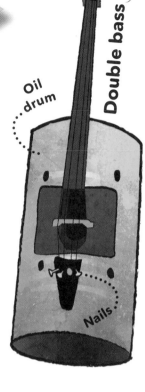

Spaghetti maker

Double bass

Oil drum

Nails

"**The world sends us trash, we send back music.**"

Fávio Chavez

Old fork

Old tins

Wood pallet

The orchestra tours all over the world. It gives the children new experiences to motivate them to learn, and opportunities to improve their future.

Create a hand puppet from odd socks. **Make** a robot costume from a cardboard box.

45

Electronic waste

Think about your favorite devices. What happens to a smartphone or tablet once it reaches the end of its life or gets broken? Electronic waste, or e-waste, is the name given to electronic gadgets that are thrown away. The more often we upgrade our devices, the more e-waste we create.

Types of e-waste

E-waste ranges from personal items such as watches and phones, to big household appliances like fridges and freezers. They can't be thrown in the normal recycling containers and usually need to be taken to a special recycling center.

Hazardous waste
Devices can contain harmful substances such as mercury, a poison found in some batteries.

Proper disposal
Items with the "waste of electrical and electronic equipment (WEEE)" symbol must not be thrown in a normal trash can.

What should I do with it?

It takes lots of energy to make electronics. If we throw them away when we are finished with them, all of this energy goes to waste.

Pass it on
If you get a new device but your old one still works, give the old one to someone who can use it.

Fix it
If an appliance breaks, try getting it repaired. A new screen could make it as good as new!

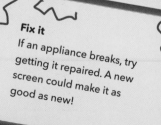

Glass is often used in phone screens. When it cracks, it can usually be replaced.

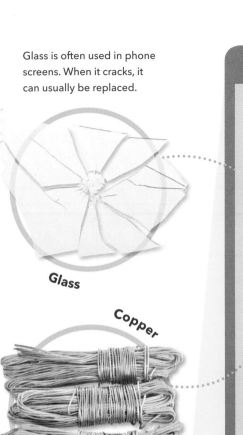

Glass

Batteries are often made of lithium metal. They can sometimes be recycled but this is expensive to do.

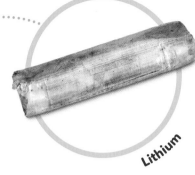

Lithium

what's in your tablet?

Tablets are very complex. They contain small amounts of lots of different precious metals, as well as rare elements like yttrium and gadolinium. These materials can be difficult to get out and reuse but it's important that we do this rather than throw them away.

Copper

Small amounts of copper are used to make wires. This can often be recycled because it's valuable.

Plastic case

A plastic case will protect your tablet, but these are difficult to recycle.

Silicon wafer

Silicon wafers can be recycled and used in solar panels.

Recycle
If it is too broken to be fixed, take it to a specialty recycling center where the parts can be used to make new electronics.

Mineral mining

Lots of the materials used in tablets and phones are difficult and dangerous to extract from the Earth. Lithium mining has been blamed for polluting water and killing fish. Valuable minerals even start wars when people fight over who controls the mines.

Food waste

Millions of people around the world are struggling to find enough food. However, in many countries, nearly a third of all food is wasted. If the amount of food we waste was given to people who needed it, then everyone would have enough to eat.

1 in 9 people in the world are going hungry for long periods of time.

20% of dairy is wasted...

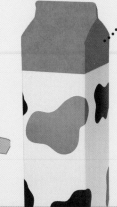

20% of meat is wasted...

30% of cereal is wasted...

30% of fish and seafood is wasted.

An estimated **45%** of lettuce in the UK is thrown away

stages of food waste

After leaving the farm, food goes through many different steps before reaching our plates. From harvesting and storage to processing and distribution, there are lots of chances for food to be wasted before it even gets to us.

8%
During collection of food, farm machinery can destroy fruit and vegetables. Crops can also be attacked by insects and disease.

8%
Poor transportation or storage can damage meat and crops. Some animals raised for meat die from diseases, making them unsafe to eat.

1.5%
When raw food is made into goods like canned foods and juices, some can be lost during the slicing, peeling, and boiling stages.

wasted resources

It takes a lot of water, energy, and farmland to produce food. When food is wasted, all of that water and energy is wasted too. If we added together all of the farmland that is used to grow food that is never eaten, it would be as big as China.

$$$

20%
of legumes are wasted.

45%
of fruit and vegetables are wasted.

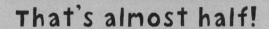

That's almost half!

In many countries, most food waste occurs in the home. Try not to buy, cook, or put on your plate more food than you really want!

4%
Food can sometimes spill inside the truck. Stores throw away fresh goods that are past their best before date.

11.5%
Lots of uneaten food in our homes, schools, restaurants, and hospitals is left on our plates and gets thrown away.

Eat up!

Have you ever put too much food on your plate and thrown leftovers away? In many countries, food that is thrown away in homes makes up more than half of all food waste. Families often buy too much and the food goes rotten before it can be eaten. However, there's lots we can do to waste less food.

Loose vegetables

Fruit and vegetables are often sold as multipacks. This means more are bought than are needed. If they're bought separately, none go to waste!

Oddly shaped

Supermarkets used to only accept nicely shaped, large fruit and vegetables. Now you can sometimes buy oddly shaped items for cheaper prices that taste just as good.

Used oil

Used cooking oil can be turned into biodiesel, a fuel used by buses in many cities.

Coffee grounds

Used coffee grounds can be placed in containers around the house to get rid of smells.

Banana bread

Brown banana

Some people don't like to eat old, brown bananas. However, they are perfect for making banana bread or ice cream.

Leftovers

Leftovers can be frozen or refrigerated in reusable containers to be enjoyed another day.

In some countries, leftover food from places such as restaurants is fed to farm animals. However, undercooked food can lead to the spread of disease among animals. Many countries have now banned this type of animal feed.

Serving size

Don't take more food than you can eat. You can always take more once you have finished!

BEST BEFORE
XX-XX-XX

Dates on food

Use by dates on food show when it becomes unsafe to eat, but best before dates show when it stops tasting its best. We can still use food after the best before date as long as it's not gone bad!

Toast was created as a way to use up stale bread!

Stale bread

If stale bread hasn't gone moldy, it can be used to make dried bread crumbs. These can be mixed with other ingredients to make sausages and other foods.

Charity box

Canned or unopened long-life food that your family doesn't use can be given to people who need it through a local soup kitchen, food bank, or homeless charity.

Bread crumbs

Sausages

Water Waste

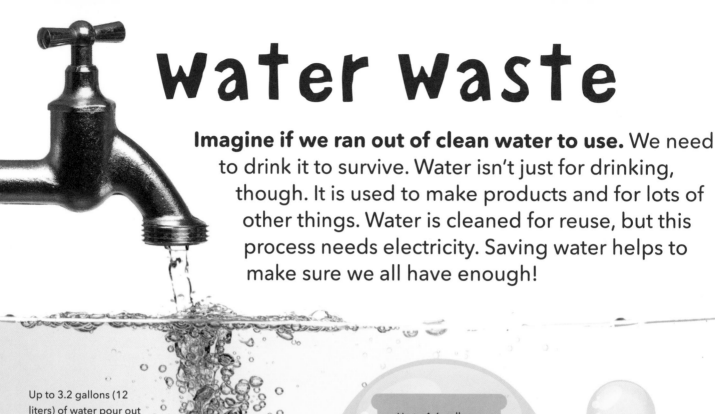

Imagine if we ran out of clean water to use. We need to drink it to survive. Water isn't just for drinking, though. It is used to make products and for lots of other things. Water is cleaned for reuse, but this process needs electricity. Saving water helps to make sure we all have enough!

Up to 3.2 gallons (12 liters) of water pour out of a running faucet a minute. Turn faucets off when you're not using them during teeth brushing and face washing.

Up to 1.6 gallons (6 liters) of water is used with one flush. In toilets with big and small flush buttons, the small button uses less water.

Water is one of our most precious resources. The amount of water on the Earth does not change and people do not have enough of it in many parts of the world.

Too much algae stops light getting to plants beneath.

Sewage

Toilet and sink waste is usually cleaned at a special center. Uncleaned sewage that gets into rivers can carry nasty poisons and diseases. These affect animals and plants. Sewage can also change water so that too much algae grows on the surface. You can write to a politician if you think there's a polluted river nearby.

We use around 80 percent of our water to grow crops. If food is wasted, even more water is needed to produce extra crops.

A cow raised for meat drinks around **15 times** the amount that humans do in a day!

A bath uses up to 21 gallons (80 liters) of water. Quick showers use much less.

Factory use

Water is required in factories to dilute chemicals, wash products, and to cool down machinery. It is also used inside lots of different products, including chemicals, food, and paper. It's important that there's enough water to keep making the products we need.

In the USA, up to **60%** of the local water supply is used to water lawns. Rain barrels can be used to collect rain for watering the yard, instead!

New car bodies are cleaned in huge tanks of water before being painted.

Hydroelectric plants use dams to create electricity.

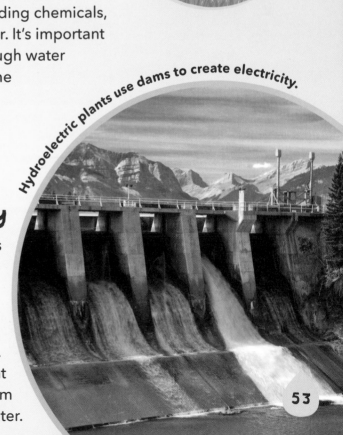

Energy

Moving water creates lots of energy that can be turned into electricity. Waves, tides, and water flowing through dams can all be used to make electricity. Norway makes 90 percent of its electricity from moving water.

1 in 9 people lacks access to safe water. Charities use donations to build wells that provide people with safe water.

where does our poop go?

Flushing the toilet

When you flush the toilet, your pee and poop gets washed into a big pipe that is full of sewage (water, pee, and poop).

Taking sewage away

Everyone poops! It's a natural part of life. In the wild, poop is recycled by tiny animals called invertebrates, and helps new plants to grow. However, we need a way to get rid of the poop from our homes, towns, and cities so it doesn't start piling up!

Bad bacteria

Fatberg

Fatbergs are solid lumps of fat found in sewers. They are made of waste that will not break down, such as cooking fat and wet wipes.

Cotton swabs

Diapers

1 in 3 people on the planet don't have a clean and private bathroom they can use.

Animal poop!

Pets poop too! As pet owners, we are in charge of getting rid of their poop responsibly so they don't spread disease and make our homes stinky.

Doggie poop

Dog poop can be dangerous to people and other animals. Collect it using biodegradable poop bags and throw it in the special dog poop trash.

Separating the waste

The water goes to a sewage plant to be treated until it is clean again. First, it is run through a giant sieve, which takes out the big bits of waste that shouldn't be there, such as diapers and cotton swabs.

Sewage treatment plant

Items that shouldn't have been flushed, such as diapers, are removed—but often things like bricks and bottles are found in sewage!

Water-treatment tanks

Good bacteria

Removing the poop

Next, the wastewater is stored in a big tank, where the poop settles to the bottom and is removed. Air can be bubbled through the water to help good bacteria grow, which kills the bad bacteria.

Sludge

Cleaning the water

In the next tank, the water is sieved through a bed of sand, and all the good bacteria settles to the bottom. The material that settles to the bottom of the tank is called sludge.

Sludge

The clean water is then returned to rivers and streams, or directly to the sea.

Sludge treatment

Most of the sludge left over from water treatment is used in farming as fertilizer. However, it can also be burned to make heat, electricity, or gas.

Cat poop

Cats poop in a litter box. Litter made from clay or silica can be very bad for the environment, so why not try one made from recycled newspaper instead?

Poop in the wild

Many insects need poop to survive! Some insects, such as dung beetles, eat it. Dung beetles even lay their eggs in a burrow full of poop!

In some countries, such as the USA, chicken poop is collected and sold as a cheap food source for beef cows.

Factories

When factories make new products, such as toys or furniture, they also produce lots of waste. This includes chemicals such as acid and bleach, scrap metal, and polluted water.

Power and chemical plants

Power plants that make electricity and chemical plants that create chemicals can produce dangerous waste, such as nuclear waste. This must be treated very carefully so it doesn't cause harm to people and animals.

Waste world

It's not just in our homes that we create trash. Huge piles of waste come from places such as factories and hospitals. Much of this waste is recycled, incinerated, or sent to landfill. However, some of it has to be treated in very special ways to make sure it doesn't cause damage to people, animals, or the environment.

Building sites

Constructing and destroying buildings causes lots of waste. Much of it comes from building materials such as bricks, concrete, wood, and tiles.

Farming, forestry, and fishing

When crops are harvested, the parts of the plant that are not sold become waste. This includes things like rice husks, the stalks of cotton plants, and coconut shells.

Mining and quarrying

We often have to dig up huge amounts of rock to get very small amounts of valuable minerals such as gold or coal. When the minerals have been taken out, big piles of waste rock are left behind.

Town and city services

Keeping our towns clean produces waste. This can be anything from the trash cleaned up off the streets to grass cuttings from the local park.

Medical buildings

Hospitals and doctors' offices produce waste that comes from treating disease. Their waste may contain drugs, surgical tools, and even body parts!

10% of global waste comes from households.

Stores

A lot of the waste produced by stores comes from the packaging their goods are delivered and sold in.

90% of waste is from elsewhere.

Fashion

We don't often think about how our clothes were made or what will happen to them once they become old or holey. Millions of clothes are thrown away every day. These could be given away or recycled instead. Materials and dyes used to make clothes can also harm the environment.

Plastic clothing

Polyester is a material found in many clothes. It sheds tiny pieces of plastic called microfibers that pollute oceans.

It takes 841 gallons (3,182 liters) of water to make one cotton shirt.

Fur

Real animal fur is used to make clothes. This comes from animals such as foxes.

Leather

Leather is made from animal skin. Chemicals and minerals are used to change skin into leather. These can be bad for the environment.

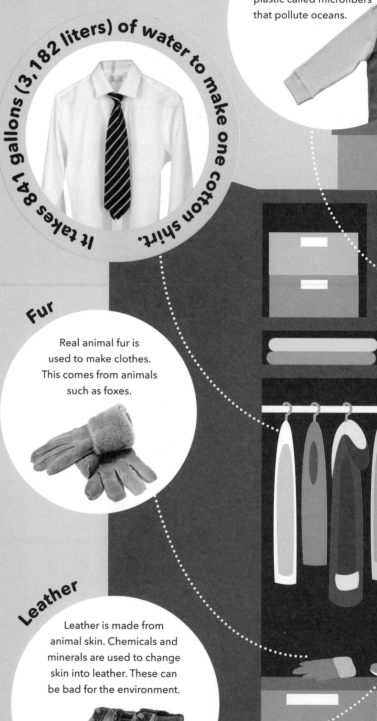

Chemical colors

Toxic chemicals can be used to create bright colors. These can leak from factories into rivers.

Girl and boy colors?

Colors can be seen as girly or boyish. Pink tops might be trashed instead of being given to little brothers!

Shoes can take up to 1,000 years to break down.

Fast fashion

Today, most clothes are sewn together in factories staffed by hundreds of people, and shipped into stores. It is easy and cheap to produce clothes, so they are sold at low prices. People therefore buy lots and throw away lots.

Ethical fashion item

Clothes such as jeans can be made out of natural materials and dyes, which break down fully in the environment.

High fashion

Many people buy more clothes than they need to keep up with changing fashions.

More than 500,000 marble-sized or larger pieces of trash are orbiting the Earth.

In 2017, there were 308,984 recorded times when space trash nearly hit other objects. More junk in space could make future space travel too dangerous.

Fishing for trash

We need to work out inventive ways of removing junk from space. In the future, satellites with nets could be used to catch it and bring it back to the Earth.

Space waste

It's not just the Earth we're covering in garbage. We have even left waste in space! Thousands of pieces of human-made trash orbit, or circle, our planet. From old satellites and dropped astronaut gloves to flecks of spacecraft paint, this junk can travel 10 times faster than a bullet and cause huge damage to spacecraft.

Large debris

Larger pieces of trash, such as abandoned rocket launch vehicles, must be recorded and tracked so that spacecraft can avoid them. In 2018, there were more than 20,000 tracked pieces of large trash.

ISS

The huge International Space Station (ISS) has to be steered out of the way of space junk around once a year. As more junk is added to space, the ISS may need to make more of these tricky moves.

Small debris

There are millions of pieces too small to be tracked, traveling at speeds of up to 17,500 mph (28,163 kph)! At these speeds, even marble-sized debris can punch holes in spacecraft.

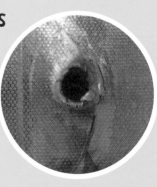

Our future planet

In 2018, there are around 7.6 billion people on our planet. By the year 2050, it will be home to nearly 10 billion. We have the power to decide what kind of world those people will live in. Will we change our habits and start to clean up the mess we have made? Or will we continue with our polluting ways?

Plastics
We're on track to be throwing away a trillion plastic bottles a year by 2021. That's enough to stretch to the moon and back, every year!

Garbage planet

If we continue adding to landfills at the same speed as we do now, they could grow taller than the Great Pyramids of Egypt. Imagine tourists flying around the world to look at piles of old trash!

Deforestation
If we continue to cut down trees at the current rate, in 100 years there will be no rain forests left. Some of the world's most beautiful and fascinating creatures could be lost forever.

Oceans
Packaging made from seaweed could replace plastic and wouldn't harm fish that nibble on it.

By the year

2050,
there will be more pieces of plastic in the ocean than fish.

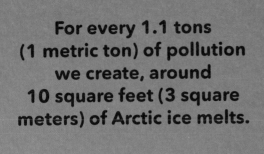

For every 1.1 tons (1 metric ton) of pollution we create, around 10 square feet (3 square meters) of Arctic ice melts.

Melting ice
Many low-lying countries, such as the Maldives, will disappear under the sea if temperatures continue to rise and more of the Arctic ice melts.

E-waste
Only tiny amounts of gold are used in laptops and phones. However, between 2018 and 2078, we will have thrown away enough to build a solid gold Eiffel Tower.

In the

8 years

between 2018 and 2025, people are set to use the same amount of plastic as in the entire 20th century.

Energy sources
The Earth's fossil fuels will eventually run out. This means that we will have to rely on other sources of energy, such as renewables.

The future is waste

It's not too late to clean up our act. Waste technology is evolving all the time, and scientists and engineers are always coming up with new ways to help us reduce and recycle our waste.

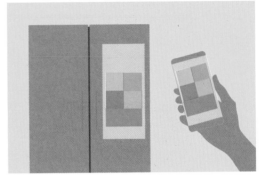

Smart fridge Your refrigerator will tell you when to use up old food so it doesn't go to waste. It might even suggest a recipe you could try!

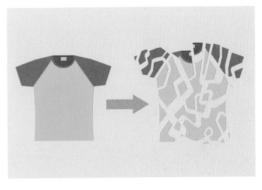

Biodegradable clothing Clothes made of natural fibers like hemp and flax could be thrown onto the compost heap when they get holes in them.

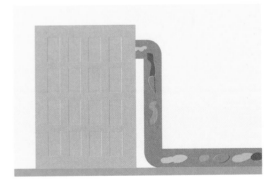

Garbage chutes Specially designed garbage chutes could carry waste all the way from the home or office to the sorting center, so we would no longer need polluting garbage trucks.

...ak to your school

...ur teachers to make changes to ...waste less as a school. Paper and ...d stock can be reused for craft ...jects. You could make a school ...ost heap or organize a swap shop ...ld clothes. You could even ask to ...eak about waste in an assembly.

Email a politician

Politicians help to make laws that affect waste, such as banning free plastic bags in stores. You can write to a local or national politician to ask them to help the environment through laws.

You have the power to make a positive change.

Be a plastic-free family

For one week, collect all of your family's plastic waste. At the end of the week, go through each item and think of plastic-free items you could use instead. By making swaps to create less waste, you can get on your way to becoming a plastic-free family!

Organize a litter-picking day

Choose a public place such as a beach or park and form a group to collect as much litter as you can find. Compete with each other to find the weirdest piece of trash, but make sure to avoid sharp objects! Ask an adult to safely get rid of these.

Find out more...

Here are a list of organizations and charities that can provide more information and ideas of how you can get involved.

Beat the Microbead

www.beatthemicrobead.org
Encourages people to avoid using products containing microplastics. An app enables you to scan a product to see if it contains them.

Freecycle

www.freecycle.org
A nonprofit organization that encourages people to give away the items they no longer need but are too good to throw away, to help reduce landfill waste.

Keep America Beautiful

www.kab.org
A national nonprofit organization that educates communites to take action to improve and beautify their communal environments.

Foodwise

www.foodwise.com.au/
A campaign run by Australian organization DoSomething! that provides people with tips and information about how they can reduce their food waste.

Friends of the Earth

www.foe.org
A group of charities from 75 different countries that work together to defend and promote environmental causes.

National Audubon Society

www.audubon.org
A nonprofit organization dedicated to promoting conservation to protect birds and the places they need to survive and thrive.

National Wildlife Federation

www.nwf.org
A national organization that works to protect and conserve wildlife and their habitats across the United States.

Ocean Conservancy

www.oceanconservancy.org
A nonprofit organization that works to create solutions to maintain a healthy ocean and a safe environment for marine wildlife.

Sierra Club

www.sierraclub.org/home
Environmental organization that aims to protect the USA's wild places and public land from pollution and destruction.

Social Plastic

www.socialplastic.org
A charity created to support and grow recycling communities to encourage recycling and prevent ocean plastic waste.

Surfrider Foundation

www.surfrider.org
A US charity that is dedicated to protecting the coastline and oceans from pollution, because it is making surfers sick.

Tree City USA

www.arborday.org
A program from the Arbor Day Foundation that promotes planting trees in urban areas to create healthy urban tree canopies.

Rainforest Alliance

www.rainforest-alliance.org.
A nonprofit organization that is dedicated to working with farmers, scientists, communities, and businesses to conserve biodiversity and ensure sustainable livelihoods.

Waste No Food

www.wastenofood.org.
A nonproift food waste charity that helps redistribute leftover food to those who need it.

World Wildlife Fund

www.worldwildlife.org
A worldwide charity that strives to protect and conserve nature and animals from pollution and deforestation.

Glossary

bacteria
Microbes that live everywhere on the Earth, such as inside food, soil, or the human body

biodiversity
The different plants and animals living in an area

climate change
Change in temperature and weather across the Earth that can be natural or caused by human activity

conservation
Protecting environments and plant and animal life

decompose
When a material or dead plant or animal breaks down naturally

E-waste
Electronic waste, such as tablets and smartphones

eco-friendly
Something that does not harm the environment

ecosystem
Living things in a particular environment that rely on one another—for example, for food or shelter

endangered
Species, or type of animal or plant, low in numbers that could become extinct

energy
Power that makes things happen. It is found in different forms, including heat, light, movement, sound, and electricity

environment
Area in which plants or animals live

extinction
When a species, or type, of animal or plant dies out completely

fossil fuels
Fuels made from animals or plants that died millions of years ago—for example—coal

glacier
Frozen river of ice that moves very slowly across land

global warming
When temperatures rise all around the world

greenhouse gas
Gas that traps heat, like a greenhouse

groundwater
Water beneath the ground

habitat
Natural home or environment of an animal

incineration
Burning something—for example, waste—in a process that may produce electricity

keystone species
Living thing that is one of the most important within an ecosystem

leachate

Water that has absorbed substances from the materials it has passed through, such as trash in a landfill

marine

Related to seas or oceans

microbes

Tiny living things that can only be seen with a microscope

ozone

A form of the gas oxygen found in a layer around the Earth, which stops too much ultraviolet light reaching the surface

poacher

Someone who kills animals without permission from the person who owns the animal or the land on which it lives

pollution

Something harmful that gets into the air, a water source, or soil

preservative

Substance added to food that keeps the food fresher for longer

renewable

Type of fuel or energy that won't run out, such as wind, or of which more can be made or grown, such as trees

resource

Something that is useful to humans, such as materials with which we can build our homes

sustainable

Use of resources in such a way that they will not run out or become too hard to find

toxic

Substance that is dangerous, such as poison

ultraviolet (UV)

Type of light that can damage human and other animal skin if the skin is exposed to it for too long

Index

Acknowledgments

DK would like to thank the following:

Caroline Hunt for proofreading; Hilary Bird for indexing; Abigail Luscombe and Seeta Parmar for editorial assistance; Sadie Thomas, Xiao Lin, Bettina Myklebust Stovne, Rachael Parfitt Hunt, and Anna Lubecka for the illustrations; Rebecca Warren for Americanization; Neeraj Bhatia, Mrinmoy Mazumdar, and Sahni Seepiya for hi-res assistance.

References:

pp40-41: Eunomia Research & Consulting and the European Environmental Bureau **pp48-49:** © FAO 2018, SAVE FOOD: Global Initiative on Food Loss and Waste Reduction, http://www.fao.org/save-food/en/, 2018

The publisher would like to thank the following for their kind permission to reproduce their photographs:

(Key: a-above; b-below/bottom; c-center; f-far; l-left; r-right; t-top)

2-3 iStockphoto.com: Worradirek (Background). **2 Dreamstime.com:** Romikmk (bl); Alfio Scisetti / Scisettialfio (cl, br). **3 123RF.com:** Roman Samokhin (bc, tr). **Dorling Kindersley:** Quinn Glass, Britvic, Fentimans (cr). **Dreamstime.com:** Aperturesound (tl). **4-5 iStockphoto. com:** Stellalevi (Background). **6 Getty Images:** Peter Macdiarmid (cl). **7 123RF.com:** photobalance (br). **8 123RF.com:** sauletas (cr). **8-9 iStockphoto.com:** Stellalevi (Background). **9 iStockphoto.com:** Dhoxax (crb); pigphoto (cb). **10-11 iStockphoto.com:** Stellalevi (Background). **11 Dreamstime.com:** Songquan Deng (bl). **12 Dreamstime.com:** Torsakarin (cl). **13 Depositphotos Inc:** urfingus (c). **Dreamstime.com:** Razvan Ionut Dragomirescu (crb); Photka (tc). **14-15 iStockphoto.com:** Stellalevi (Background). **14 123RF.com:** Eric Isselee / isselee (br). **15 Getty Images:** Mamunur Rashid / NurPhoto (bl). **NASA:** Goddard Scientific Visualization Studio (cr, fcr). **16-17 iStockphoto.com:** Stellalevi (Background). **16 Dreamstime.com:** Dolphfyn (bl); Andrey Gudkov (br). **iStockphoto.com:** Bogdanhoria (t). **17 iStockphoto.com:** Yotrak (t). **18-19 Dreamstime.com:** Stockbymh (t). **18 Fotolia:** Eric Isselee (crb). **iStockphoto.com:** Stellalevi (t/Background). **19 123RF.com:** Sergey Krasnoshchokov / most66 (br). **Alamy Stock Photo:** Avalon / Photoshot License (cr); Hemis (tr). **Dreamstime.com:** Johannes Gerhardus Swanepoel (c). **iStockphoto.com:** Alasdair Sargent (cl). **20 Dreamstime.com:** Artjazz (br); Nostal6ie (tr). **21 123RF.com:** Johann Ragnarsson (cl); Valery Shanin (bl); Nerthuz (br, fbr). **Dreamstime.com:** Delstudio (cla). **22 iStockphoto.com:** Kenneth Taylor (br); Wysiati (crb). **23 Alamy Stock Photo:** Arcaid Images (clb); James Davies (bl). **24 123RF.com:** Roman Samokhin (cb); Anton Starikov (crb). **Dorling Kindersley:** Quinn Glass, Britvic, Fentimans (cb/Glass bottle). **Dreamstime.com:** Aperturesound (fcra); Dmitry Rukhlenko (cra); Romikmk (clb). **25 123RF.com:** photobalance (fclb); Anton Starikov (cb). **Dreamstime.com:** Alfio Scisetti / Scisettialfio (clb). **26 Dreamstime.com:** Rangizzz (clb). **26-27 Dreamstime.com:** Maria Luisa Lopez Estivill (b). **27 Dreamstime.com:** Ilfede (crb); Ulrich Mueller (cra); Vchalup (cr); Huguette Roe (clb). **28-29 Getty Images:** Santirta Martendano / AFP. **29 Getty Images:** David Rubinger / The LIFE Images Collection (tr); PhotoStock-Israel (crb). **30 Dreamstime.com:** Alfio Scisetti / Scisettialfio (br). **31 123RF.com:** Aleksey Poprugin (tc, fcr); Roman Samokhin (cra). **Dreamstime.com:** Alfio Scisetti / Scisettialfio (t, fbr). **32 Dorling Kindersley:** Museum of Design in Plastics, Bournemouth Arts University, UK (cb). **Dreamstime.com:** Alfio Scisetti / Scisettialfio (ca). **iStockphoto.com:** MentalArt (cl); t3000 (cla). **33 123RF.com:** Monica Boorboor / honjune (br). **Dorling Kindersley:** Museum of Design in Plastics, Bournemouth Arts University, UK (cb). **Dreamstime.com:** Jo Ann Snover / Jsnover (ca). **iStockphoto.com:** likstudio (crb); Yurdakul (tr). **34-35 123RF.com:** Roman Samokhin (ca). **34 123RF.com:** Aleksey Poprugin (cr). **Dorling Kindersley:** Quinn Glass, Britvic, Fentimans (ca). **Dreamstime.com:** Alfio Scisetti / Scisettialfio (cra). **35 123RF.com:** Aleksey Poprugin (clb); Roman Samokhin (c/Can). **Alamy Stock Photo:** Paulo Oliveira (crb). **Dorling Kindersley:** Quinn Glass, Britvic, Fentimans (c, clb/Bottle). **Dreamstime.com:** Alfio Scisetti / Scisettialfio (ca). **iStockphoto.com:** CasarsaGuru (cl). **36 Alamy Stock Photo:** ZUMA Press, Inc. (bc). **Dreamstime.com:** Arun Bhargava (br). **iStockphoto.com:** kali9 (cr); SolStock (cl). **36-37 Dreamstime.com:** Jetanat Chermchitrphong (Background). **37 Dreamstime.com:** Katie

Nesling (cl). **iStockphoto.com:** vgajic (cb). **The Ocean Cleanup:** (cla, ca). **38-39 iStockphoto.com:** Stellalevi (Background). **38 123RF.com:** Aleksey Poprugin (cr). **40-41 iStockphoto.com:** Stellalevi (Background). **40 123RF.com:** Anton Starikov (c). **Dreamstime.com:** (cb/Boxes); Alfio Scisetti / Scisettialfio (ca); Stocksolutions (cra). **iStockphoto.com:** dejanj01 (b); grimgram (cb). **41 Dreamstime.com:** Alfio Scisetti / Scisettialfio (cl). **42 123RF.com:** jemastock (c). **Dreamstime.com:** Alfio Scisetti / Scisettialfio (clb); Tom Wang (cb). **43 Dreamstime.com:** Igor Zakharevich (tc). **44 Dreamstime.com:** Winai Tepsuttinun (tl). **Getty Images:** Norberto Duarte / AFP. **45 Alamy Stock Photo:** Everett Collection Inc (b). **46 123RF.com:** cobalt (cb); szefei (cb/Forest). **Dreamstime.com:** Jf123 (crb); Nerthuz (clb); Liouthe (cb/Camera); Nikolai Sorokin (fcrb). **47 123RF.com:** Anton Burakov (cra/Plastic case); Sergey Sikharulidze (clb/Ebook); scanrail (c). **Alamy Stock Photo:** Africa Media Online (br). **Dorling Kindersley:** RGB Research Limited (cra). **Dreamstime.com:** Andrey Popov (clb); Wissanustock (cla). **48 Dreamstime.com:** Lunamarina (cr). **iStockphoto.com:** Coprid (cl). **49 123RF.com:** Monica Boorboor / honjune (cr); Евгений Косцов (br). **Dreamstime.com:** Lunamarina (ca); Alexander Pladdet / Pincarel (fcra, c, cb). **iStockphoto.com:** Coprid (cb/Dairy box); Stellalevi (Background). **50 Dreamstime.com:** Varnavaphoto (cl, c). **51 Dreamstime.com:** Steven Cukrov / Scukrov (bl). **52-53 iStockphoto.com:** Pterwort. **52 123RF.com:** Pumidol Leelerdsakulvong (bc). **53 123RF.com:** Eric Isselee / isselee (tr). **Alamy Stock Photo:** Cultura Creative (RF) (cl). **Dreamstime.com:** Supertrooper (cr). **iStockphoto.com:** Androsov (br); YinYang (tl). **54-55 123RF.com:** andreykuzmin (bc). **iStockphoto.com:** Stellalevi (Background). **55 Dreamstime.com:** Neal Cooper / Cooper5022 (bc); Josefkubes (cla); Theo Malings (br). **56 123RF.com:** Kirill Kirsanov (cla). **Dreamstime.com:** Buriy (ca); Lightzoom (fcla); Tat'yana Mazitova (fcra); Alexander Levchenko (cra); Photka (bc/Sand); Anton Starikov (bc/Metal nut); Cherezoff (br). **Fotolia:** Vadim Yerofeyev (bc). **57 123RF.com:** Kanlaya Chantrakool (ca/Rice grains); shaffandi (ca); imagemax (ca/Apple). **Dreamstime.com:** Henrik Dolle (fcrb); Rsooll (cla); Sarah Marchant (clb); Alexander Pladdet / Pincarel (c); Yury Shirokov / Yuris (c/Batteries); Sinisha Karich (crb). **58 123RF.com:** Igor Zakharevich (ca). **Dreamstime.com:** Denys Kovtun (bc); Yulia Gapeenko / Yganko (cb); Tetiana Zbrodko (cra). **59 123RF.com:** mawielobob (cla); pixelrobot (ca); Vitalii Tiahunov (bc). **Dreamstime.com:** Ruslan Gilmanshin (ca/Pink tshirt); Milos Tasic / Tale (cra, crb). **60-61 iStockphoto.com:** johan63; Stellalevi (Background). **61 NASA:** (br); NASA's Eyes on the Earth 3D (cra). **62 123RF.com:** Boris Stromar / astrobobo (tr); Aleksey Poprugin (cr); Yotrak Butda (bc). **Dorling Kindersley:** Jerry Young (fcrb, crb). **Dreamstime.com:** Steve Mann (clb); Alfio Scisetti / Scisettialfio (tr/Bottles); Onyxprj (cra). **62-63 Dreamstime.com:** Onyxprj (c/Bottles); Alfio Scisetti / Scisettialfio (c). **64-65 iStockphoto.com:** Stellalevi (Background). **66-67 iStockphoto.com:** Stellalevi (Background). **68-69 iStockphoto.com:** Stellalevi (Background). **70 123RF.com:** Aleksey Poprugin (fbr/Bag); Roman Samokhin (fbr). **Dorling Kindersley:** Quinn Glass, Britvic, Fentimans (br). **Dreamstime.com:** Alfio Scisetti / Scisettialfio (fbl). **71 123RF.com:** Roman Samokhin (crb). **Dorling Kindersley:** Quinn Glass, Britvic, Fentimans (bc). **Dreamstime.com:** Alfio Scisetti / Scisettialfio (bl)

Cover images: Front: 123RF.com: Aleksey Poprugin bc, Roman Samokhin clb; **Dorling Kindersley:** Quinn Glass, Britvic, Fentimans bl; **Dreamstime.com:** Penchan Pumila / Gamjai cla, cb, Alfio Scisetti / Scisettialfio (Bottles); Back: **123RF.com:** Aleksey Poprugin bl, Roman Samokhin clb, cr; **Dorling Kindersley:** Quinn Glass, Britvic, Fentimans clb/ (Glass bottle); **Dreamstime.com:** Alfio Scisetti / Scisettialfio (Bottles)

All other images © Dorling Kindersley
For further information see:
www.dkimages.com